# The 99 Names of Allah Acquiring The 99 Divine Qualities of God

# Copyright information

Kadmon, Baal

The 99 Names of Allah- Acquiring the 99 Divine Qualities of God

−1st ed

Printed in the United States of America

Cover image : #66202594 © Saida Shigapova- Fotolia.com
Book Cover Design: Baal Kadmon

# INTRODUCTION

"Allah has ninety-nine names, i.e. one-hundred minus one, and whoever knows them will go to Paradise." - Sahih Bukhari Book 50 Hadith Qudsi 894

In the first volume of the **Sacred names series** : "The 72 Names of God: The 72 keys to Transformation" I discuss the power of the name. Knowing a name gives you power.

In this book we will discuss the 99 names of Allah, what they are, and how to use them to instill in yourself with the power of God.

Throughout the mystical traditions of the world, several traditions stand out as luminaries. One of these luminous traditions is Sufism. Sufism is the mystical tradition of the Muslim faith. Like any spiritual tradition, mystical interpretations are often hinted at in the main body of religious texts, but other books are needed to decipher the inner mysteries of an established canon. This applies to Islam as well.

Islam's main holy book is the Quran. A beautifully written and deep tome. Often , in the west we do not see the depth of Islam because it has been shrouded in the deeds of a few radical people who have lost the true spirit of the Quran. This is a shame because the Quran is quite a deep book.  It is much more  than a book on how to conduct ones life. It is a manual for divine enlightenment.  Its deeper mysteries are hidden in the text and voluminous works like the Hadith are used to tease them out.  In the Hadith it discusses the 99 names of God. These names are essentially 99 qualities that God possess. These names are meant as guides in our own life. If you have ever seen picture of Muslims holding beads in their hands , those beads are used to chant the 99 names of Allah. This tradition is very much embedded in Islamic tradition.

In this book, we will learn how to tap into the 99 names of Allah and acquire the 99 divine qualities.

# Chapter 1: The Significance Of The 99 Names Of Allah

According to the traditions of Islam, the prophet Mohammed used several names to called upon God. Most of these names can be found in the Quran and a few others in the extracanonical texts of Islam called the Hadith. Although technically there are more than 99 names throughout these texts. The 99 names or the Asma Allah al-husna are considered special. The great Sufi Mystic Ibn Arabi stated that the 99 names of Allah are the outward signs of the inner most mysteries of all creation. It is for this reason I have written this book. To tap into their amazing power.

When these names are recited you are tapping into the very essence of the name and power of God. But not only that, there are other benefits of chanting these names. They can bring about dramatic change in your life.

I will present to you now all 99 names in transliterated English, Arabic and their general meaning. In the next chapter I will go deeper into the practice and how these names can help you. I will also include the pronunciations as well.

# The 99 Names of Allah:

1. Al Rahman     الرحمن     The Most Compassionate

2. Al Raheem     الرحيم     The Most Merciful

3. Al Malik     الملك     The Sovereign Ruler

4. Al Quddus     القدوس     The Most Sacred

5. Al Salaam     السلام     The Source of Peace

6. Al Mu'min     المؤمن     The Source of Faith

7. Al Muhaymin     المهيمن     The Guardian

8. Al 'Azeez     العزيز     The Almighty

9. Al Jabbaar     الجبار     The Powerful

10. Al Mutakabbir     المتكبر     The Dominant One

11. Al Khaaliq     الخالق     The Creator

12. Al Baari'     البارئ     The Maker

13. Al Musawwir     المصور     The Fashioner of Forms

14. Al Ghaffar     الغفار     The Great Forgiver

15. Al Qahhaar     القهار     The All Compelling Subduer

| 16. | Al Wahhaab | الوهاب | The Bestower |
| 17. | Al Razzaaq | الرزاق | The Ever Providing |
| 18. | Al Fattaah | الفتاح | The Opener |
| 19. | Al 'Aleem | العليم | The All Knowing |
| 20. | Al Qaabid | القابض | The Restrainer, the Straightened |
| 21. | Al Baasit | الباسط | The Expander |
| 22. | Al Khaafid | الخافض | The Abaser |
| 23. | Al Raafi' | الرافع | The Exalter |
| 24. | Al Mu'izz | المعز | The Giver of Honor |
| 25. | Al Mudhill | المذل | The Giver of Dishonur |
| 26. | Al Samee' | السميع | The All Hearing |
| 27. | Al Baseer | البصير | The All Seeing |
| 28. | Al Hakam | الحكم | The Judge |
| 29. | Al 'Adl | العدل | The Just |
| 30. | Al Lateef | اللطيف | The Kind |
| 31. | Al Khabeer | الخبير | The All Aware |
| 32. | Al Haleem | الحليم | The Forbearing |
| 33. | Al 'Azeem | العظيم | The Magnificent and the Infinite |

| 34. | Al Ghafur | الغفور | The All Forgiving |
|---|---|---|---|
| 35. | Al Shakur | الشكور | The Grateful |
| 36. | Al 'Alee | العلى | The Exalted |
| 37. | Al Kabeer | الكبير | The Great |
| 38. | Al Hafeez | الحفيظ | The Preserver |
| 39. | Al Muqeet | المقيت | The Nourisher |
| 40. | Al Haseeb | الحسيب | The Reckoner |
| 41. | Al Jaleel | الجليل | The Majestic |
| 42. | Al Kareem | الكريم | The Bountiful |
| 43. | Al Raqeeb | الرقيب | The Watchful |
| 44. | Al Mujeeb | المجيب | The Responsive |
| 45. | Al Waasi' | الواسع | The all encompassing |
| 46. | Al Hakeem | الحكيم | The Wise |
| 47. | Al Wadoud | الودود | The Loving |
| 48. | Al Majeed | المجيد | The All Glorious |
| 49. | Al Baa'ith | الباعث | The Raiser of the Dead |
| 50. | Al Shaheed | الشهيد | The Witness |
| 51. | Al Haqq | الحق | The Truth, the Real |

| 52. | Al Wakeel | الوكيل | The Dependable |
|---|---|---|---|
| 53. | Al Qawiyy | القوى | The Strong |
| 54. | Al Mateen | المتين | The Firm |
| 55. | Al Walee | الولى | The Helper |
| 56. | Al Hameed | الحميد | The All Praiseworthy |
| 57. | Al Muhsee | المحصى | The Accounter |
| 58. | Al Mubdee' | المبدئ | The Originator |
| 59. | Al Mu'eed | المعيد | The Reinstater Who Brings Back All |
| 60. | Al Muhyee | المحيى | The Giver of Life |
| 61. | Al Mumeet | المميت | The Bringer of Death, the Destroyer |
| 62. | Al Hayy | الحي | The Ever Living |
| 63. | Al Qayyoum | القيوم | The Self Subsisting Sustainer of All |
| 64. | Al Waajid | الواجد | The Perceiver |
| 65. | Al Maajid | الماجد | The Magnificent |
| 66. | Al Waahid | الواحد | The One, the All Inclusive |
| 67. | Al Samad | الصمد | The Self Sufficient |
| 68. | Al Qaadir | القادر | The All Able |
| 69. | Al Muqtadir | المقتدر | The All Determiner |

| 70. | Al Muqaddim | المقدم | The Expediter |
| 71. | Al Mu'akhkhir | المؤخر | The Delayer |
| 72. | Al Awwal | الأول | The First |
| 73. | Al Akhir | الأخر | The Last |
| 74. | Al Zaahir | الظاهر | The Manifest |
| 75. | Al Baatin | الباطن | The Hidden |
| 76. | Al Waalee | الوالي | The Patron |
| 77. | Al Muta'aalee | المتعالي | The Self Exalted |
| 78. | Al Barr | البر | The Most Kind and Righteous |
| 79. | Al Tawwaab | التواب | The Ever Returning |
| 80. | Al Muntaqim | المنتقم | The Avenger |
| 81. | Al 'Afuww | العفو | The Pardoner |
| 82. | Al Ra'uf | الرؤوف | The Compassionate |
| 83. | Malik al Mulk | الملك مالك | The Owner of All Sovereignty |
| 84. | Dhu al Jalaal | الجلال ذو | The Lord of Majesty |
| 85. | wal Ikraam | الإكرام و | and Generosity |
| 86. | Al Muqsit | المقسط | The Equitable |
| 87. | Al Jaami' | الجامع | The Gatherer |

| | | | |
|---|---|---|---|
| 88. | Al Ghanee | الغنى | The All Rich |
| 89. | Al Mughnee | المغنى | The Enricher, the Emancipator |
| 90. | Al Maani' | المانع | The Withholder |
| 91. | Al Daarr | الضار | The Distressor |
| 92. | Al Naafi' | النافع | The Benefactor |
| 93. | Al Nour | النور | The Light |
| 94. | Al Haadee | الهادئ | The Guide |
| 95. | Al Badee' | البديع | Incomparable |
| 96. | Al Baaqee | الباقي | The Ever Enduring |
| 97. | Al Waarith | الوارث | The Heir, |
| 98. | Al Rasheed | الرشيد | The Guide |
| 99. | Al Sabour | الصبور | The Patient |

# Chapter 2: Invoking The 99 Names Of Allah

In this chapter will invoke the 99 names of Allah. You will see that these 99 names not only bestow the qualities on you but they can also help you with your physical as well as spiritual needs. I will format each name as follows.

I will provide the Arabic letters

The Pronunciations

The benefits of chanting each name.

The personal powers you will gain

When invoking the names, please follow the steps below.

**1. Find The Name you want to resonate with.**

**2. Look at the name**

**3. Chant the name as many times as you want, This can be audible or in your mind**

**4. Take a Deep breath and go about your day. You may chant the name or names as many times as you want.**

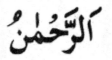

## ARE-RAHMAN

**BENEFIT:** By reciting this name, you can free yourself from depression.

**Personal power you will gain:** You will become more merciful towards others

# NAME 2

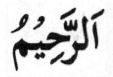

## ARE-RAH-HEEM

**BENEFIT:** By reciting this name, you will gain the friendship of others. This will also protect you from harm

**Personal power you will gain:** You will become more giving.

# NAME 3

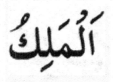

## AL-MA-LEEK

**BENEFIT:** By reciting this name, you will gain financial abundance

**Personal power you will gain:** You will become more giving.

# NAME 4

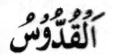

## AL-KOODS

**BENEFIT:** By reciting this name, you can free yourself from depression and anxiety.

**Personal power you will gain:** You will gain inner sanctity

## NAME 5

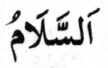

### AS-SA-LAM

**BENEFIT:**  By reciting this name, you can heal the sick

**Personal power you will gain:** You will gain inner peace

# NAME 6

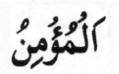

## AL-MOO-MEEN

**BENEFIT:** By reciting this name, you will be protected from all harm

**Personal power you will gain:** You will live in faith

# NAME 7

الْمُهَيْمِنُ

## AL-MOO-HI-MEEN

**BENEFIT:** By reciting this name, you will gain holiness of Body, Mind and Spirit

**Personal power you will gain:** You will gain holiness

# NAME 8

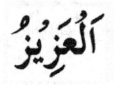

## AL-AZIZ

**BENEFIT:** By reciting this name, you will gain self sufficiency and independence from others

**Personal power you will gain:** You will gain inner motivation

# NAME 9

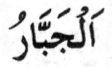

## AL-JABAR

**BENEFIT:** By reciting this name, you will gain power over all circumstances in your life

**Personal power you will gain:** You will gain great inner strength

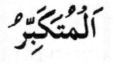

## AL-MOO-TAKA-BEER

**BENEFIT:** By reciting this name, you will gain the respect of others and success in all endeavors.

**Personal power you will gain:** You will gain charisma

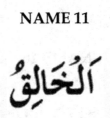

## اَلْخَالِقُ

## AL-KAH-LEAK

**BENEFIT:** By reciting this name, you will gain merits of heaven

**Personal power you will gain:** You will gain spiritual righteousness

# NAME 12

## AL-BA-RI

**BENEFIT:**  By reciting this name, you will attract order into your life

**Personal power you will gain:** You will gain orderliness and have the ability to endure chaotic events

# NAME 13

اَلْمُصَوِّرُ

## AL-MOOSA-WEER

**BENEFIT:**  By reciting this name, you will cure infertility

**Personal power you will gain:** You will gain material manifestation abilities.

# NAME 14

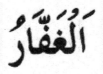

## AL-GA-FAR

**BENEFIT:** By reciting this name, you will be forgiven of your sins

**Personal power you will gain:** You will gain a forgiving disposition

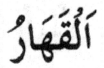

## AL-KAH-HAR

**BENEFIT:** By reciting this name, you will liberate your mind from material things

**Personal power you will gain:** You will eradicate greed in you

# NAME 16

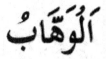

## AL-WA-HAB

**BENEFIT:** By reciting this name, you will liberated from poverty.

**Personal power you will gain:** You will gain the ability to alleviate poverty in others.

## ARE-RA-ZAQ

**BENEFIT:** By reciting this name, you will never want for anything

**Personal power you will gain:** You will gain the ability to manifest

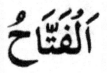

## AL-FA-TAH

**BENEFIT:** By reciting this name, you will open your heart

**Personal power you will gain:** You will gain the ability to be compassionate

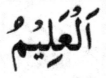

## AL-ALEEM

**BENEFIT:** By reciting this name, you will discern divine secrets

**Personal power you will gain:** You will gain the ability to be channel of God

## AL-KA-BEED

**BENEFIT:**  By reciting this name, you will never go hungry

**Personal power you will gain:** You will gain faith in divine providence

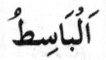

## AL-BA-SEAT

**BENEFIT:** By reciting this name, you will never need others to sustain you

**Personal power you will gain:** You will gain inner conviction and strength

# NAME 22

الُخَافِضُ

## AL-KA-FEED

**BENEFIT:** By reciting this name, you will defeat those who are against you

**Personal power you will gain:** You will gain the ability to ward off enemies

**ARE-RA-FEE**

**BENEFIT:** By reciting this name, you will gain status and recognition

**Personal power you will gain:** You will gain the ability to handle stress and status gracefully

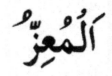

## AL-MOO-EASE

**BENEFIT:**  By reciting this name, you will  become fearless

**Personal power you will gain:** You will gain courage in the face of all people and adversity

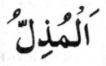

## AL-MOOD-HEAL

**BENEFIT:** By reciting this name, you will divert the evil energies of those who are envious of you

**Personal power you will gain:** You will eradicate jealousy in your heart

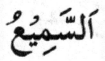

## AS-SAMMY

**BENEFIT:** By reciting this name, you will be able to manifest anything you ask of God

**Personal power you will gain:** You will be directly linked to God

# NAME 27

اَلْبَصِيرُ

## AL-BA-SEER

**BENEFIT:** By reciting this name, you will gain enlightenment

**Personal power you will gain:** You will be instilled with inner spiritual light

# NAME 28

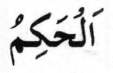

## AL-HA-KAM

**BENEFIT:**  By reciting this name, you will learn the secrets of the Universe

**Personal power you will gain:** You will have the ability to teach the mysteries

# NAME 29

## AL-ADILL

**BENEFIT:**  By reciting this name, you will gain control over others

**Personal power you will gain:** You will have the ability to be persuasive

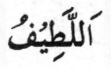

## AL-LA-TEEF

**BENEFIT:** By reciting this name, you will gain control over your life circumstances

**Personal power you will gain:** You will have the ability to come up with solutions to your problems

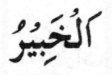

**AL-KAH-BEER**

**BENEFIT:** By reciting this name, you will gain control over and eradicate your bad habits

**Personal power you will gain:** You will have willpower of steel

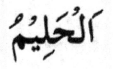

## AL-HA-LEAM

**BENEFIT:** By reciting this name, you will be protected from natural disasters

**Personal power you will gain:** You will have power to remove evil from everywhere that you go

# NAME 33

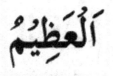

## AL-AZEEM

**BENEFIT:** By reciting this name, you will be respected

**Personal power you will gain:** You will have power to draw people to you

# NAME 34

الْغَفُورُ

## AL-GA-FOOR

**BENEFIT:** If you are sick and have a headache, this name will help you

**Personal power you will gain:** You will have power to heal yourself

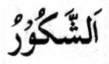

## ASH-SHA-KOOR

**BENEFIT:** By reciting this name, all your financial problems
will go away

**Personal power you will gain:** You will have power to have
what it takes to make money in this world

# NAME 36

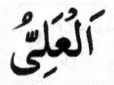

## AL-ALI

**BENEFIT:** By reciting this name, you will gain respect and success in your endeavors

**Personal power you will gain:** You will have power to attract your desires

# NAME 37

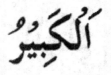

## AL-KA-BEER

**BENEFIT:**  By reciting this name, you will win in games of chance or in politics

**Personal power you will gain:** You will have power to attract good luck

# NAME 38

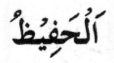

## AL-HA-FEES

**BENEFIT:** By reciting this name, you will be protected from harm

**Personal power you will gain:** You will have power to attract good fortune

# NAME 39

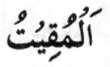

## AL-MOO-KEET

**BENEFIT:** By reciting this name, your children will be obedient

**Personal power you will gain:** You will have power to calm people

# NAME 40

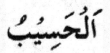

## AL-HA-SEEB

**BENEFIT:** By reciting this name, your problems will resolve in your favor

**Personal power you will gain:** You will have power to go communicate directly with God

اَلْجَلِيلُ

## AL-JA-LEEL

**BENEFIT:** By reciting this name, you will be well liked by others

**Personal power you will gain:** You will have natural social abilities

# NAME 42

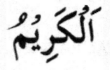

## AL-KA-REEM

**BENEFIT:** By reciting this name, you will achieve spiritual esteem

**Personal power you will gain:** You will have spiritual peace in your heart

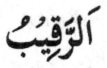

## AL-RA-KEEB

**BENEFIT:** By reciting this name, you will gain divine protection from all bad things

**Personal power you will gain:** You will have power to avert crisis

# NAME 44

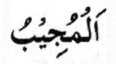

## AL-MOO-JEEB

**BENEFIT:** By reciting this name, you will have all your prayers answered **be careful what you ask for**

**Personal power you will gain:** You will have powerful prayers

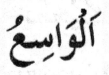

## AL-WA-SEE

**BENEFIT:** By reciting this name, you will find it easy to get a job

**Personal power you will gain:** You will have inner harmony with material success.

اَلْحَكِيمُ

## AL-HA-KEEM

**BENEFIT:** By reciting this name, you will gain true wisdom

**Personal power you will gain:** You will have the power to reach peoples and help them spiritually

# NAME 47

الْوَدُودُ

## AL-WA-DUDE

**BENEFIT:** By reciting this name, you will reconcile with your significant other

**Personal power you will gain:** You will have the power to achieve harmonious relationships

# NAME 48

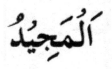

## AL-MA-JEED

**BENEFIT:** By reciting this name, you will gain glory in life

**Personal power you will gain:** You will glow with power and glory. People will notice you.

# NAME 49

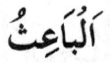

## AL-BA-IT

**BENEFIT:**  By reciting this name, you will become God fearing

**Personal power you will gain:** You will have a humble spirit

# NAME 50

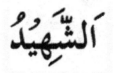

## ASH-SHA-HEED

**BENEFIT:** By reciting this name, you will attract harmony in your relationships

**Personal power you will gain:** You will have the power to help people reach a state of equilibrium emotionally

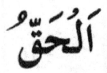

## AL-HUK

**BENEFIT:** By reciting this name, you will find lost objects

**Personal power you will gain:** You will gain more
dependability in your life

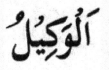

## AL-WA-KEEL

**BENEFIT:** By reciting this name, you will be protected from bodily harm

**Personal power you will gain:** You will gain the power and strength to save people from harm

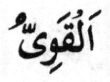

## AL-KA-WEE

**BENEFIT:** By reciting this name, you will be free from those who want to harm you

**Personal power you will gain:** You will gain the inner resources you need to stand up for yourself

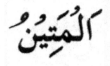

## AL-MA-TEEN

**BENEFIT:** By reciting this name, you will have no worries in this life

**Personal power you will gain:** You will gain the inner strength to endure any hardship

## AL-WA-LEE

**BENEFIT:** By reciting this name, you will gain divine favor

**Personal power you will gain:** You will gain the Midas touch

# NAME 56

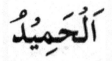

## AL-HA-MEED

**BENEFIT:** By reciting this name, you will be loved by all

**Personal power you will gain:** You will gain charm and influential abilities

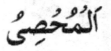

## AL-MOOH-SEE

**BENEFIT:**  By reciting this name, you will gain heaven

**Personal power you will gain:** You will gain righteousness

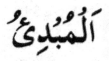

## AL-MOOB-DEE

**BENEFIT:** By reciting this name, you will have a child

**Personal power you will gain:** You will gain powers to bestow fertility on yourself and others

# NAME 59

ٱلْمُعِيدُ

## AL-MOO-EED

**BENEFIT:** By reciting this name, you will be protected in your travels

**Personal power you will gain:** You will have your prayers answered

# NAME 60

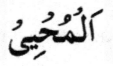

## AL-MOO-HAYA

**BENEFIT:** By reciting this name, you will be relieved of your burdens

**Personal power you will gain:** You will have the power to relieve the suffering of others

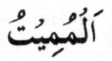

## AL-MOO-MEET

**BENEFIT:** By reciting this name, you will destroy your enemies **(Use With Caution)**

**Personal power you will gain:** You will have the power to repel your enemies

# NAME 62

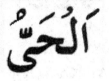

## AL-HY

**BENEFIT:** By reciting this name, you will achieve longevity

**Personal power you will gain:** You will have the habits to lead a healthy life

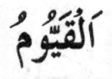

## AL-KA-YOOM

**BENEFIT:** By reciting this name, you will avoid misfortune

**Personal power you will gaim:** You will have the ability to attract only good things to your life

# NAME 64

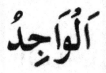

## AL-WA-JEED

**BENEFIT:** By reciting this name, you will have a joyous heart

**Personal power you will gain:** You will have the ability to live a joyous life.

# NAME 65

اَلْمَاجِدُ

## AL-MA-JEED

**BENEFIT:** By reciting this name, you will attain divine revelation

**Personal power you will gain:** You will have the ability to commune with angels

اَلْوَاحِدُ

## AL-WA-HEED

**BENEFIT:** By reciting this name, you will be free of fear

**Personal power you will gain:** You will be fearless

# NAME 67

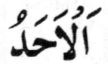

## AL-AH-HAD

**BENEFIT:** By reciting this name, you will glean universal secrets

**Personal power you will gain:** You will be a conduit of divine knowledge

# NAME 68

الصَّمَدُ

## AL-SA-MAD

**BENEFIT:** By reciting this name, you will have people looking to you for guidance

**Personal power you will gain:** You will be a conduit of knowledge that will help others

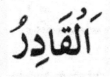

## AL-KA-DEER

**BENEFIT:** By reciting this name, you will manifest your heart's desire

**Personal power you will gain:** You will be a powerful manifester

# NAME 70

اَلْمُقْتَدِرُ

## AL-MOOK-TA-DEER

**BENEFIT:** By reciting this name, you will know the truth about everything

**Personal power you will gain:** You will be a discerner of the truth

# NAME 71

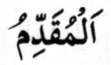

## AL-MOOK-AH-DEEM

**BENEFIT:**  By reciting this name, if you are in the military, this name will protect you

**Personal power you will gain:** You will always have protective energy about you

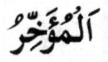

## AL-MOOK-KA-HEAR

**BENEFIT:** By reciting this name, you love of God will be complete

**Personal power you will gain:** You will always have divine energy emanating from your heart

## AL-AWAL

**BENEFIT:** By reciting this name, you will banish infertility

**Personal power you will gain:** You will always have creative energy

# NAME 74

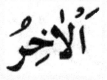

## AL-ACHIR

**BENEFIT:** By reciting this name, you will lead a fulfilled life

**Personal power you will gain:** You will always have good luck energy around you

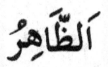

## AZ-ZAHEER

**BENEFIT:**  By reciting this name, you will be given divine
light

**Personal power you will gain:** You will always have divine
energy around you and people will be drawn to you

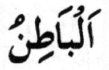

## AL-BA-TEEN

**BENEFIT:** By reciting this name, you will never be in the dark about anything

**Personal power you will gain:** You will always have the upper hand in your affairs

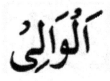

**AL-WA-LEE**

**BENEFIT:** By reciting this name, you will bring protective energies in your house

**Personal power you will gain:** You will always feel safe

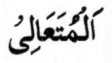

**AL-MOOT-ALI**

**BENEFIT:** By reciting this name, you will have God benevolence

**Personal power you will gain:** You will have God energy about you

## AL-BAR

**BENEFIT:**  By reciting this name, you will insure your children will be successful

**Personal power you will gain:** You can will yourself into having healthy and happy children at the moment of conception

# NAME 80

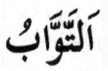

## AL-TA-WAB

**BENEFIT:**  By reciting this name, your sins will be forgiven

**Personal power you will gain:** You will always be introduced to events that will increase our spirituality

# NAME 81

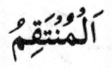

## AL-MOON-TAKIM

**BENEFIT:** By reciting this name, your enemies will fall away

**Personal power you will gain:** You will always have good luck in competitions or business

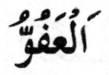

## AL-AFOO

**BENEFIT:** By reciting this name, your sins will be forgiven

**Personal power you will gain:** You will always be introduced to events that will increase our spirituality

# NAME 83

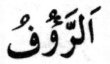

## AL-RA-OOF

**BENEFIT:** By reciting this name, you will always be blessed

**Personal power you will gain:** You will always be blessed and it will emanate from you.

مَالِكُ الْمُلْكِ

## MALIK-UL-MOOLK

**BENEFIT:** By reciting this name, you will gain esteem amongst your peers

**Personal power you will gain:** You will always exude confidence

# NAME 85

ذُوالْجَلَالِ وَالْاِكْرَامِ

## DOOL-JA-LA-LEE-WAL-IKRAM

**BENEFIT:** By reciting this name, you will gain wealth beyond belief

**Personal power you will gain:** You will be a powerful manifester of money

# NAME 86

اَلْمُقْسِطُ

## AL-MOOK-SEAT

**BENEFIT:**  By reciting this name, you will banish all evil spirits

**Personal power you will gain:** You will be able to control and repel evil entities

# NAME 87

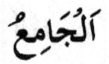

## AL-JAH-MEE

**BENEFIT:** By reciting this name, you will find any lost object

**Personal power you will gain:** You will never be absent minded again

# NAME 88

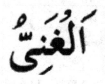

## AL-GA-HANI

**BENEFIT:** By reciting this name, you will never feel envy and jealousy again

**Personal power you will gain:** You will always be content with life

# NAME 89

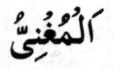

## AL-MUG-HANI

**BENEFIT:** By reciting this name, you will never need anyone else help

**Personal power you will gain:** You will always be self sufficient

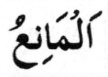

## AL-MANI

**BENEFIT:**  By reciting this name, you will have a happy
family life

**Personal power you will gain:** You will always attract
harmonious relationship with your family

# NAME 91

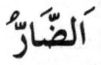

## AD-DAR

**BENEFIT:**  By reciting this name, you will have tranquility in your life

**Personal power you will gain:** You will always attract harmonious situations in your life

# NAME 92

## AN-NA-FEE

**BENEFIT:** By reciting this name, before an endeavor, you will be successful

**Personal power you will gain:** You will always attract success in your endeavors and projects

# NAME 93

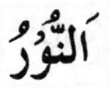

## AN-NOOR

**BENEFIT:** By reciting this name, you will gain inner light

**Personal power you will gain:** You will always be illuminated

# NAME 94

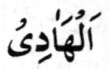

## AL-HADI

**BENEFIT:** By reciting this name, you will be free of all wants and needs

**Personal power you will gain:** You will always be provided for

## AL-BA-DEE

**BENEFIT:** By reciting this name, you will be free of distressing events

**Personal power you will gain:** You will always be in beneficial situations

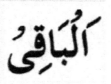

**AL-BA-KEY**

**BENEFIT:** By reciting this name, you will be guided to do good deeds

**Personal power you will gain:** You will always be in state of generosity of spirit

# NAME 97

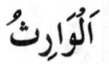

## AL-WA-REET

**BENEFIT:** By reciting this name, you will be cure of depression

**Personal power you will gain:** You will always be able to shift more positive mindset

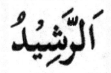

## AR-RASHEED

**BENEFIT:** By reciting this name, you will always know how to proceed in your endeavors

**Personal power you will gain:** You will always be decisive

اَلصَّبُوْرُ

## AL-SABOOR

**BENEFIT:** By reciting this name, you will always get out of a bind

**Personal power you will gain:** You will always find a way out of your ruts

# ALLAH

# Conclusion

We have come to the end of this text. I know that many of the names seem to do the same thing. Despite that, I would experiment with them and see how they work for you. This book was for general use and not set in stone. You can try these names with different scenarios in your life .

I am confident that by simply doing these exercises with the 99 names of Allah, you will gain great benefit. They are, after all, Gods Name.